Grades 5-6
Learner Resource

Year Blue, Semester 1

By Tanya Ferdinandusz

This learner resource is accompanied by the Grades 5-6 Teacher Guide and the Grades 5-8 Teacher Class Kit.

Editors: Arlene Flancher, Jill Carroll Lafferty, and Julie Lindesmith
Designers: Chance•Nelson, Inc.; Kristine Mudd
Illustrators: Pamela Johnson and Kristine Mudd

ISBN 0-8066-4765-5

Sunday School Curriculum

Contents

1	In the Garden	2
2	O Brother!	6
3	Battle of the Brothers	10
4	Good Out of Bad	14
5	The Top Ten	18
6	Beautiful Inside	22
7	Who's the Wisest of Them All?	26
8	Fire!	30
9	After the Bath	34
10	In High Places	38
11	Follow the Shepherd	42
12	Jonah's Decision	46
13	Joy to the World	50
14	John Is Born	54
15	The Christ of Christmas	58
	Map	62
	What's in a Name?	64

Augsburg Fortress
www.augsburgfortress.org

Manufactured in U.S.A.
2 3 4 5 6 7 8 9 0 1 2 3 4 5 6 7 8 9

How Does Your Garden Grow?

If you could create your ideal garden, what would it be like? Would you give it a name? Where is your favorite outdoor place? What do you like about it? What do you do there? Who do you spend time with in this place? Draw a picture of your favorite outdoor place or your ideal garden, or write a poem about it.

Digging In

How might you feel if you did something wrong and someone found out?

How might you feel if someone you love wronged you?

Bible Text
Genesis 3

Key Verse And the man and his wife hid themselves from the presence of the Lord God among the trees of the garden.
Genesis 3:8

2

SEQUENCES & Consequences

How did the serpent persuade Eve to eat the fruit? (Genesis 3:1-5).

What did Adam and Eve do after they had eaten the fruit? How did they feel? (Genesis 3:7-13).

What did God do after Eve and Adam ate the fruit? (Genesis 3:14-24)

Bible Connections

Through the Bible's stories, we discover the importance of obeying God. What can we learn about obedience from these verses?

Matthew 7:24-25
John 14:15
Exodus 20:1-7

Witness WORDS

sin: turning away from God, disobeying God, rebelling against God

tempt: to coax or persuade someone to do something wrong

FAITH Traits

obedience In the Bible: How do you think Adam and Eve felt when they realized God knew they had been disobedient? In your own life: Who (or what) tempts you to disobey God? What do you do?

BIG Idea

God cares about what we do.

Surprising Grace

Imagine that you are a parent. Your son or daughter has been invited to go to a movie with friends. The house rule is simple: if homework is done, going to a movie is fine. Your child lies about having homework finished and goes to the movie anyway. How might you respond with grace?

You Write the Script
What does it mean to:

Resist temptation

Take responsibility for our mistakes

Apologize

Accept consequences

BRAIN Builders

Artists
Draw a cartoon strip for today's story.

Nutritionists
First, describe the nutritional value of the fruit that Adam and Eve ate, then explain why it was not good for them to eat it.

Snake Charmers
Make and decorate a snake, then use it to retell today's story from the snake's perspective.

witnesses in the world

God cares about what you do. What will you do or say in each of the situations below?

TAKE iT HOME

How can you resist temptation at school? At home? With friends?

<< Looking Back

How did God care for Adam and Eve?
How does God care for you?

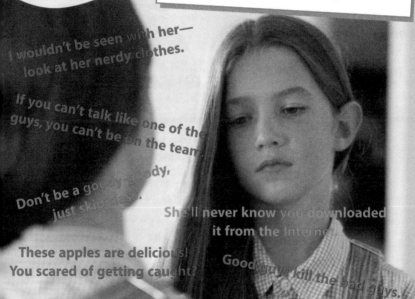

I wouldn't be seen with her— look at her nerdy clothes.

If you can't talk like one of the guys, you can't be on the team.

Don't be a goody-goody, just skip class.

She'll never know you downloaded it from the Internet.

These apples are delicious! You scared of getting caught?

Good guys kill the bad guys.

Closing Prayer

Creator God, we praise you for the beautiful world you created for us to enjoy. Help us to listen to your voice and obey you. Amen

Better THAN Yours

Have you ever had a disagreement with a brother or sister?

Have you experienced jealousy? When?

What do you do when you feel jealous and angry toward a family member? A friend?

FAITH Traits

forgiveness *In the Bible:* Cain was angry and jealous of Abel. What happened when God confronted Cain?

In your own life: When you are questioned about a specific negative behavior, what do you do?

DIGGING IN

Who might say…
  That's not the right answer.
  Foul!
  Stop! First beat the eggs, then add flour.
  That chord didn't sound right.
How do you feel when someone points out something that is your mistake?
How do you react—what do you say or do?

Bible Text
Genesis 4:1-16

Key Verse And the Lord put a mark on Cain, so that no one who came upon him would kill him.
Genesis 4:15

Bible Connections

How did the people in these stories react when confronted with their wrongdoing?

Adam & Eve (Genesis 3:8-13)
David (2 Samuel 12:1-12)
Peter (Matthew 26:69-75)

What does 1 John 1:8-9 say about sin and forgiveness?

BIG Idea

God knows we need to be forgiven.

SPELL IT OUT

What was it that Cain needed? Solve the word puzzle below to find out.

Clue	Answer
Cain's job	FARMER
Relationship between Cain and Abel	BROTHERS
Cain's offering to God	FRUIT
When his offering wasn't accepted, Cain was ____	ANGRY
Cain ____ Abel!	KILLED
Abel's mother's name	EVE
God asked Cain, "Where is ____ ?"	ABEL
The land Cain moved to	NOD
Cain said to God, "Am I my brother's ___ ?"	KEEPER
Abel's job	SHEPERD
God ____ Cain because he killed Abel.	PUNISHED

Farmers and Shepherds

Fill in the blanks with "Cain" or "Abel."

Abel was a shepherd.

Cain was a farmer.

TAKE iT HOME

Think of times at home and at school when you get angry, and remember that God is with you even then!

UPROOTING!

Think of one sin you would like to uproot from your life, then imagine pulling it out like you would pull a weed out of the ground. God knows we all need forgiveness.

BRAIN Builders

Actors Perform a skit about a fifth or sixth grader who is jealous because his or her best friend does really well in math.

Doctors Give a humorous lecture about the symptoms of and treatment for anger.

Word Pros Make as many words as you can out of the word *FORGIVENESS*.

Game Lovers Play the Character game.

witnesses
in the
world

The world is full of warnings about all kinds of things. What kinds of warning messages do you read and hear about health? Safety? The environment?

What happens when these warnings are ignored?

What happens when they are followed?

DANGER!

D + ANGER = DANGER!

FEELING ANGRY IS NOT A SIN, BUT HOLDING ANGER INSIDE ISN'T GOOD FOR ANYBODY! WHAT DOES THE BIBLE SAY ABOUT ANGER?

EPHESIANS 4:26-27
EPHESIANS 4:31-32
MATTHEW 5:21-25

WHAT MIGHT YOU DO DIFFERENTLY THE NEXT TIME YOU'RE ANGRY?

Witness **WORDS**

sacrifice: an offering (usually animals or grain) to God

<<Looking Back

How did Cain respond to God's questions about where Abel was? How did God respond to Cain? Is there forgiveness in this story?

Closing **Prayer**

Lord, help me to uproot anger, jealousy, and hatred from my life. Help me learn to ask for forgiveness. Amen

DIGGING IN

Talk about a time when you believe a parent or teacher favored someone over you. How did you feel? Have you ever been in a situation when those around you were doing something wrong and somebody spoke out against it? What happened?

Family

Family members have times when they get along, and times when they don't. When do you get along best with your family members? When is it most difficult? Have you ever had to stand up for someone in your family?

Bible Text
Genesis 37:12-36

Key Verse Reuben said to them, "Shed no blood; throw him into this pit here in the wilderness, but lay no hand on him"—that he might rescue him out of their hand and restore him to his father. Genesis 37:22

BIG Idea
God wants us to stand up for others.

FAITH Traits

boldness *In the Bible:* Which of Joseph's brothers stood up for him and tried to save him?
In your own life: How can you act with courage and boldness? Has anyone ever acted boldly for you?

Bible Connections

The Bible is full of stories of men and women who were bold in their faith.
Read Acts 3:1-10; 4:13-22, 31 and learn about the courage and boldness of Peter and John.

Jealous of Joseph

Joseph was a teenager from a large family. His father, Jacob, loved him very much and gave him a special long-sleeved coat to wear. Joseph had dreams of greatness, and his brothers grew to be very jealous of him. What happened next?

Genesis 37:12-17
Genesis 37:18-22
Genesis 37:23-24
Genesis 37:25-28
Genesis 37:29-31
Genesis 37:32-36

Stand Up!

Suggest a bold course of action for each of the situations described below:

A new kid is getting bullied by nearly everyone in the class...

You are at a sleepover, and your friends are watching a movie that you know your parents would object to...

Your friends want to copy your math homework and threaten to drop you from the group if you refuse...

TAKE IT HOME

Think of one person you can stand up for this week, at home, at school, or in your neighborhood. Pray for boldness to do what is right.

BRAIN Builders

Detectives
Ishmaelites, descendants of Ishmael, purchased Joseph for 20 pieces of silver. Use your powers of observation and deduction to figure out more about Ishmael. (Hint: Read Genesis 16:15-16; 17:18-20.) Who was he? Who were his father and his mother?

Clothing Designers
Make a paper pattern for Joseph's beautiful long-sleeved robe.

Game Lovers
Play the Faith Traits game.

witnesses in the world

People all over the world support those in need in all kinds of ways. Work with your friends to figure out ways to care for others in your community. Choose an idea from this list, or think of something else.

Donate food to a food shelf.

Donate clothing or blankets to a homeless shelter.

Donate children's books to a safe haven for kids.

Pray for crime victims.

Witness WORDS

tearing one's clothes: a way of showing deep sorrow, despair, or mourning

Pharaoh: the Egyptian king or ruler

<< Looking Back

Who tried to kill Joseph?
Who stood up for him?
Where was Joseph taken?

Closing Prayer

Lord, help me to be bold in standing up for what is right, knowing that you are with me always and will help me. Amen

4 Good Out of Bad

Two men look out through the same bars:

One sees the mud, and one the stars.

—Frederick Langbridge (1849-1923)

WHAT DO YOU SEE?

Tell about a time when you looked out the window and saw something quite different from what everyone else was seeing.

FAITH Traits

forgiveness *In the Bible:* Why do you think Joseph forgave his brothers?
In your life: Have you ever been hurt by a friend or family member? What do you feel like doing when that happens? If you follow Joseph's example, what might you decide to do?

Bible Text
Genesis 45:1-15; 50:15-21

Key Verse Even though you intended to do harm to me, God intended it for good. Genesis 50:20

Big Idea

Forgiveness leads to love.

Bible Connections

What do you learn about forgiveness from each of these passages? Read them and give each passage an appropriate title.

Psalm 103:8-14
Matthew 18:21-22
Matthew 6:12

Dream Come True

Joseph lived and worked in Egypt for many years. His family lived in Canaan. During a severe famine in Canaan, Joseph's brothers traveled to Egypt seeking food, and they found something completely unexpected.

Unscramble the words in quotation marks below and learn what Joseph said when he saw his brothers for the first time in many years. (Refer to Genesis 45:4 if you need to!)

Then Joseph said to his brothers, "closer me to come." And they came closer. He said, "brother sold am whom Egypt Joseph into your you I."

How does the story end?

What did Joseph do when his brothers asked for forgiveness? (Genesis 50:16-17)

What did Joseph say? (Genesis 50:19-21)

DIGGING IN

What was the best dream you ever had? How did you feel about it when you woke up? What was the worst dream you ever had? How would you feel if that dream came true?

Mud or Stars?

Read Frederick Langbridge's quote on page 14. What are some "stars" (good things) you might find in each of the situations described below?

* Your very best friend moves away

* You hurt your leg and can't play in the next game

* You don't get a part in the school play

TAKE IT HOME

This week, choose to forgive someone who has hurt or harmed you, and experience God's healing love!

WORDS

dreams: in Biblical times, God often spoke to people through dreams

famine: a serious shortage of food for a group of people

BRAIN Builders

Mathematicians
Using Genesis 37:2 and Genesis 41:46, calculate roughly how many years Joseph was in Egypt.

Bookworms
Talk about a book that tells the story of brothers or sisters. In what ways is the family in your book like Joseph and his family? In what ways are they different?

Dreamers
Draw a picture of your favorite dream, then describe it to a friend.

<<Looking Back

Did Joseph choose forgiveness or revenge?
How did his brothers react when they realized they were forgiven?
Is it possible to trust God even when bad things happen in your life?

Sorry!

Think about what "sorry" really involves.

S earch your heart

O wn up to your mistake and ask for forgiveness

R esolve to make things right

R epair damaged relationships or things

Y ield yourself to God

When is it hard to say "I'm sorry"?
What does it feel like to apologize?

witnesses
in the
world

Name some situations in the world where forgiveness is needed.

In your own life, where can you offer forgiveness?

Closing Prayer

Forgive us our sins, Lord, and help us to forgive those who hurt us. Amen

WHICH BOOK?

What kinds of books might have these instructions and rules?

Add a spoonful of sugar and beat well.

Press CTRL-U to underline text.

fff is a triple forte, which means to play or sing loudly!

Are instructions and rules helpful? Why or why not?

BIG Idea

God helps us do what is right.

DIGGING IN

Who do you think is best qualified to guide each of these situations?

SURGERY

FOOTBALL GAME

ORCHESTRA PRACTICE

PLAY REHEARSAL

LIFE

TRAFFIC JAM

Bible Text
Exodus 19:16-25; 20:1-17

Key Verse I am the Lord your God, who brought you out of the land of Egypt, out of the house of slavery.
Exodus 20:2

THE TEN COMMANDMENTS

MOSES WENT TO THE TOP OF MOUNT SINAI AND RECEIVED THE TEN COMMANDMENTS FROM GOD. WHICH COMMANDMENTS ARE ABOUT OUR RELATIONSHIP WITH GOD? WHICH HELP US WITH OUR RELATIONSHIPS WITH OTHERS?

1. I am the Lord your God. You shall have no other Gods.

2. You shall not make wrongful use of the name of the Lord your God.

3. Remember the Sabbath day, and keep it holy.

4. Honor your father and your mother.

5. You shall not murder.

6. You shall not commit adultery.

7. You shall not steal.

8. You shall not bear false witness against your neighbor.

9. You shall not covet your neighbor's house.

10. You shall not covet anything that belongs to your neighbor.

Bible Connections

Read Matthew 22:36-40. According to Jesus, what are the two greatest commandments?

FAITH Traits

obedience In the Bible: Obedience is a choice. Do you think the Israelites chose to obey the Ten Commandments all the time? In your own life: When is it easy to choose to obey God? When is it hard?

YOU SHALL **NOT MURDER.**

ADVERTISING
God's Commandments

Create an advertisement or slogan that encourages others to follow the Ten Commandments. What will you say?

BRAIN
Builders

Actors
Choose one of the commandments and create a two-part skit. In the first part, break the commandment you have chosen, and in the second part, show how to obey it.

Lawmakers
Make up rules (both DOs and DON'Ts) for something you think is important (protecting the environment, safe schools, and so forth).

Game Lovers
Play the Character game; this time, explain how the character kept or broke one of God's commandments.

Witness

WORDS

Egypt: an African country where the Israelites were slaves before God sent Moses to set them free

Mount Sinai: a mountain in present-day Saudi Arabia; the place where Moses received the Ten Commandments

TAKE iT HOME

As you watch TV or read books and magazines this week, look for people keeping or breaking the Ten Commandments.

What is your favorite TV show?

Describe an incident from this show where a character keeps or breaks one of the Ten Commandments. What are the consequences?

witnesses in the world

<<Looking Back

Jesus summarized the Ten Commandments given to Moses in two simple statements. What are they? Love _____. Love _____. (Hint: Look up Matthew 22:36-40.)

Closing Prayer

Lord, thank you for giving us wise rules for life. Help us to keep your rules and make our world a better, safer, and happier place. Amen

6 Beautiful Inside

LOOK AGAIN!

What do you see? Now look again…and again…and again! Do you see anything different? There's more than one way of looking at something or someone.

Has a teacher or a coach ever noticed something about you that your family members never saw? Have you recognized something in a person that nobody else has? In today's story, God sees something in someone that nobody else does.

DiGGiNG In

Imagine that your teacher (or coach) announces that one student is going to be chosen for a very special and important task.

How might you feel if you were chosen?

How might you feel if you were NOT chosen?

Bible Text
1 Samuel 16

Key Verse For the Lord does not see as mortals see; they look on the outward appearance, but the Lord looks on the heart. 1 Samuel 16:7

Israel's first king, Saul, displeased God, so God sent the prophet Samuel to Bethlehem to anoint a new king.

Read 1 Samuel 16:1-23, and discover more about this story.

How did Samuel feel about God rejecting King Saul? (verse 1)

Where did Jesse live? (verses 1, 4)

How many sons did Jesse have? (verses 10-11)

David was Jesse's _____ son. (verse 11)

What was David doing when Samuel and Jesse were visiting? (verse 11)

What did David look like? (verse 12)

What happened to Saul? (verse 14)

What did David play to help Saul feel better? (verse 23)

NEXT, Please!

✝ Bible Connections

King David was from Bethlehem. What New Testament person was born in Bethlehem? (Hint: Read Luke 2:1-7.) Is there a connection between King David and this person?

BIG Idea

Anyone can be called to serve God.

FAITH Traits

humility *In the Bible:* Who expected young David to be anointed king? Who was humble in this story?

In your own life: How might you put someone else first?

YOU COULD BE KING!

WHAT KINGLY TRAITS DO YOU HAVE?

WHAT WOULD YOU DO IF YOU WERE KING?

TAKE IT HOME

Tell all of your family members what you love about them!

BRAIN Builders

Interviewers
Pretend to be Samuel interviewing David for the job of king. What questions will you ask? How will David answer?

Singers/Rappers
Create an original song or rap about today's story.

Beauty Lovers
Describe, with words or actions, the most beautiful thing in the world. It can be a person, place, animal, or an attribute like kindness or hope.

witnesses in the world

God WaNts you to serve iN the KiNgdoM of HeaveN.

What are your taleNts?

What do you Love to do?

How caN you serve God?

God Wants You!

<< Looking Back

Who anointed David?
Who was David's father?
Was David's anointing a surprise?

Witness WORDS

prophet: a person who speaks God's message to others

horn of oil: container filled with olive oil and spices; used to anoint a new king

Closing
Prayer

Creator God, thank you for creating me in your image and likeness. Help me to grow into the beautiful person you have created me to be, loving you and serving you faithfully. Amen

Blow the Whistle!

Disputes are common and it's important to settle them quickly and fairly. Who (or what) can help you settle each of the following disputes?

"The ball was in!" "No, it was out!"

"I'm taller than you are." "No, I'm taller!"

"I did better in math." "No, I did!"

"That's not how you spell 'quarrel.'" "Yes, it is!"

"Lisa's only 11." "No, she's 12."

DiGGiNG iN

What does it mean to be wise? Do you know anyone who is wise?

Bible Text
1 Kings 3:16-28

Key Verse And they stood in awe of the king, because they perceived that the wisdom of God was in him, to execute justice.
1 Kings 3:28

Read 1 Kings 3:16-28, and try to put yourself in the story.

What might you do if you were the mother of the baby who died?

What would it be like to stand before the king?

If you were the mother of the baby who was alive, what would you do when King Solomon suggests cutting the baby in two?

Two Women and a Baby

Bible Connections

The book of Proverbs contains many wise sayings attributed to King Solomon. What does each of these proverbs say about wisdom?

Proverbs 10:21
Proverbs 13:1
Proverbs 13:10
Proverbs 15:7
Proverbs 16:16
Proverbs 16:23
Proverbs 29:8
Proverbs 29:11

FAITH Traits

wisdom *In the Bible:* Why did Solomon ask God for wisdom? *In your own life:* Is it possible to be really smart and unwise at the same time? How can you grow in wisdom?

BIG Idea

Wisdom comes from God.

It's Fair!

What are your group's golden rules for settling disputes?

GOLDEN RULES FOR SETTLING DISPUTES

1. _____
2. _____
3. _____
4. _____
5. _____

TAKE IT HOME

This week, use the golden rules from It's Fair! at home and at school.

BRAIN Builders

Game Lovers
Play the Faith Traits game.

Artists
Draw a picture of one of the scenes from today's story (for example, the happy mother and baby reunited).

Journalists
Write a front-page news story about the "case" tried by King Solomon.

WORDS

wisdom of God: viewing things from God's perspective, having an understanding mind, executing justice fairly

witnesses in the world

Countries around the world use courts of law, international tribunals, war, trade restrictions, and diplomatic talks to settle disputes.

Do you think these are good or bad ways to settle differences between countries and people?

Think of a dispute you have. How can you settle this dispute in a way that is fair to you and the other person?

<< Looking Back

Where does wisdom come from?
Why did King Solomon want to be wise?

Closing Prayer

God, please make me wise with YOUR wisdom, so that I can live peacefully and lovingly with the people in my life. Amen

Bible Text
1 Kings 18:20-39

Key Verse How long will you go limping with two different opinions? If the Lord is God, follow him; but if Baal, then follow him. 1 Kings 18:21

BIG Idea

Worship shows we love God.

Alphabet Contest

Write down as many different kinds of contests you can think of that begin with each of the following letters. (One has been done for you!)

Eating

Lemon eating

Ice cream makeing

Jogging

Amazing race

Hockey

DIGGING IN

What does it mean to be powerful?
Name some powerful people...
   At school
   In your neighborhood
   In your country
   Around the world
What powers do these people have?
What can they do?

Breaking (the Drought) News

The people of Israel worshiped other gods, particularly Baal, the Canaanite god of rain and fertility. In the story in 1 Kings 18, Elijah, the prophet, works hard to remind the Israelites that God, and not Baal, is all-powerful.

Where does this story take place? (v. 20)

How many people supported Elijah? (v. 22)

How many prophets supported Baal? (v. 22)

What kind of animal was used in the sacrifice? (v. 23)

How will the people know that God, and not Baal, is all-powerful? (vv. 23-24)

How many times is water poured on Elijah's altar? (vv. 33-35)

What happens in the end? (vv. 38-39)

If you were a news or sports broadcaster, how might you report this story?

Bible Connections

God promised Elijah that the drought would end. Read 1 Kings 18:41-45 and discover what happened at the end of today's story.

FAITH Traits

reverence In the Bible: In Elijah's time, the people were not showing reverence for God. They were running after other gods. How did Elijah show reverence?

In your own life: What does it mean to have other gods? How can you show reverence to God?

All Power Is Yours

God created a beautiful world for us to live in. Write a prayer of thanks for this world and for all of God's blessings in your life.

BRAIN Builders

Moviegoers
Talk about a movie where a "little guy" or an underdog triumphed against great odds. What did you like best about the movie?

Dancers
Use colored scarves to do a fire dance!

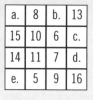

Public Speaker
Choose one side of an issue, and create a persuasive speech in an effort to get others to join your cause.

a.	8	b.	13
15	10	6	c.
14	11	7	d.
e.	5	9	16

Number Crunchers
Can you solve this magic square puzzle? The numbers in each row, in each column, and diagonally must add up to 34.

Clues:
a. number of true prophets in today's story
b. number of stones Elijah used for the altar
c. number of times Elijah poured water on the altar
d. number of bulls
e. number of water jars Elijah used

W

witnesses
in the
world

People are affected by all kinds of disasters: war, flood, famine, drought, hurricane, earthquakes, poverty, and many others. What are some disasters that currently are taking place in the world? Close to home? How can you help?

Witness WORDS

altar: a place of worship, used for sacrifices

Baal: a Canaanite god believed to be responsible for rainfall and fertility

drought: a long period of time without any precipitation

TAKE iT HOME

Decide to stand up for what is right and always speak and act in ways that honor God.

<< Looking Back

God is more powerful than anyone or anything in this universe. How did the prophets of Baal learn this? How do you know this?

Closing Prayer

Praise to God, wonderful creator of the universe. Thanks be to God for life! Amen

9 After the Bath

CALL THE DOCTOR

What would you prescribe for each of the following illnesses and ailments?

AILMENTS	CURES
FLU	SURGERY
COUGH	ANTIBIOTICS
SKIN DISEASE	AN OINTMENT
APPENDICITIS	A SYRUP
THROAT INFECTION	PLENTY OF FLUIDS AND REST

Have you ever been sick and had a doctor prescribe a course of treatment that you didn't want to follow? What did you do? Who helped you?

DIGGING IN

Think about a time when you were ill or in pain. How did you feel? Who helped you? If someone you love were very ill, how might you feel? What could you do?

Bible Text
2 Kings 5:1-19

Key Verse If only my lord were with the prophet who is in Samaria! He would cure him of his leprosy.
2 Kings 5:3

W

Bible Connections

The young girl in today's story did something extraordinary. The Gospels are full of stories about God calling ordinary people to do extraordinary things. Who does God call in each of these texts?

Mark 1:16-20
Luke 2:8-20
John 6:8-13

SAYS WHO?

Match each of the following statements with the person who might have said it:

1. Thanks a heap!
2. Madam, I've got an idea.
3. I've heard you can help me.
4. No worries—I can help him.
5. Take a bath!
6. There's hope for you, darling.
7. Your majesty, could you put in a word for me?
8. Don't be foolish and miss your big chance.

a. Naaman to the king of Aram
b. Elisha to the king of Israel
c. Slave girl to Naaman's wife
d. Servants to Naaman
e. Naaman's wife to Naaman
f. Naaman to Elisha before the healing
g. Elisha to Naaman before the healing
h. Naaman to Elisha after the healing

BIG Idea

God sends people to heal us.

FAITH Traits

compassion In the Bible: The young girl in today's story had compassion and did something to help Naaman. Who else showed compassion?
In your own life: Think of a few people you feel sorry for…how can you show active compassion?

35

Link in the Chain

Doctors and nurses help to bring healing to people, but many other people help, too. Name as many of them as you can. How do you bring healing to people?

TAKE iT HOME

Pray for the sick and suffering this week.

BRAIN Builders

Songwriters
Use a familiar tune, and make up a song that tells today's story.

Inventors
Think of a funny cure for a fake illness (*defrost a frozen shoulder in the microwave!*) and spend a few seconds justifying your choice of cure to your classmates.

Puzzle Pros
Naaman bathed in the Jordan River and was healed. Use the letters below to discover other places to get wet.

```
        J
S _ O _ _ _
    R _ _ _ R
_ O _ D
    L A _ _
_ C _ _ N
```

witnesses in the world

Who helps spread the good news of Jesus throughout the world?

How can you help spread the good news in your own corner of the world?

How about in faraway places?

<< **Looking Back**

Who told Naaman's wife that Naaman could be healed? How was Naaman healed?

Witness WORDS

leprosy: In biblical times, the term *leprosy* was used to describe a variety of different skin diseases. People with leprosy were declared spiritually unclean and were unable to participate in worship. Today, *Hansen's Disease* is the medical name for leprosy, and it can be treated with antibiotics.

Closing Prayer

Dear God, we pray for
_____, who needs
healing today. Amen

10 In High Places

Queen for a Day

Imagine you are the queen of a country that is ruled by a king. How will you fill your day? Will you be by yourself or with people? Will you stay at home? Will you work? Will you volunteer somewhere? What will you do?

10 extremely responsible

1 utterly irrresponsible

FAITH Traits

responsibility *In the Bible:* Esther didn't use her position to further her own interests. What group of people was she responsible for saving?
In your own life: Rate yourself on the responsibility scale above. (You don't have to show this to anyone!)

Bible Text
Esther 2–8

Key Verse Who knows? Perhaps you have come to royal dignity for just such a time as this. Esther 4:14

SEND MAIL

Esther was an orphaned Jewish girl who lived in the Persian Empire with her older cousin Mordecai. She was a beautiful young woman, and one day the king chose her to be his queen.

Check out these scripture references and create an e-mail correspondence between Queen Esther and Mordecai that will retell Esther's amazing story of bravery and responsibility.

Esther 2:1-2, 8
Esther 2:17-18
Esther 2:21-22
Esther 3:8-11
Esther 4:1-5
Esther 4:6-11

Esther 4:12-17
Esther 5:1-8
Esther 7:1-6
Esther 8:3-6, 8
Esther 8:15-17

✝ Bible Connections

God calls us to be responsible. Pantomime a responsible interpretation of one of these texts.

Genesis 1:26-31
1 Corinthians 12:12-26
1 Corinthians 3:16-17

DiGGiNG iN

Name some important, well-known people from history. What kinds of things did they do? Name some important, well-known people who are alive today. What do they do? Name some important not-so-well known people whom you know. What kinds of things do they do?

BIG idea

Brave believers help their friends.

Road to Responsibility

What are the MOST IMPORTANT things you do to be a responsible young person?

BRAIN
Builders

Artists
Design a bravery medal for Queen Esther.

Writers
Pretend to be a young Jewish girl or boy and write a thank-you letter to Queen Esther.

Cheerleaders
Make up a cheer to applaud Queen Esther for her courage, and perform this for the rest of the group.

Game Lovers
Play the Character game or What's the Big Idea?

witnesses
in the
world

What does it mean to be brave?
When are you brave?
When is it hard to be brave?
Can you do something brave that will help one other person?

<< Looking Back

Why do you think Queen Esther risked her safety to save the Jewish people?

Witness WORDS

scepter: a rod held in the hand of a king as a sign of authority

decree: a law or an official ruling

TAKE iT HOME

This week take time to pray for people whose lives are in danger.

Closing Prayer

Lord, help me to act more responsibly by _____. Amen

Pets

Describe your pet, or the pet you would like to have.

What do you do to care for your pet?

DIGGING IN

Who helps you when you…
• are hungry or thirsty?
• have to go somewhere?
• are sick?

• are worried?
• need information?
• have questions about God?

Psalm 23 compares God to a shepherd who takes good care of his sheep. Think of some other images describing what God is like and what God does.

FAITH Traits

peace *In the Bible:* Psalm 23 is about God's peace. What is God's peace like?
In your own life: Are you worried scared, or stressed? Jesus, the Good Shepherd, is with you always—even in times that feel chaotic and scary.

Bible Text
Psalm 23

Key Verse The Lord is my shepherd, I shall not want. Psalm 23:1

Follow the Shepherd

Imagine you are a sheep walking with Jesus, the Good Shepherd, and think of a short, catchy phrase that summarizes each line of Psalm 23. A few have been done for you.

Bi**G** I**dea**

God provides comfort and safety.

1. The Lord is my shepherd—*You're the Boss!*
2. I shall not want—*I have everything I need.*
3. He makes me lie down in green pastures—Your comfortable
4. He leads me beside still waters—He makes us drink
5. He restores my soul— he
6. He leads me in right paths for his name's sake— he steers and in right direction
7. Even though I walk though the darkest valley, I fear no evil, for you are with me— safe
8. Your rod and your staff—they comfort me— safe
9. You prepare a table before me in the presence of my enemies— be together
10. You anoint my head with oil; my cup overflows— Blessed
11. Surely goodness and mercy shall follow me all the days of my life—
12. And I shall dwell in the house of the Lord my whole life long— *Together forever!*

✝ Bible Connections

Each of these passages is about shepherds. What do good shepherds do? What should they avoid doing?

Ezekiel 34:1-16   John 10:11-18   1 Peter 5:1-4

Write a Psalm

Write a personal version of Psalm 23 based on your own life.

BRAIN Builders

Singers
Learn and memorize the song for Psalm 23 and teach it to another group of kids.

Public Speakers
Pretend to be a sheep and give a one-minute speech thanking your shepherd.

Game Lovers
Play the Faith Traits game.

TAKE IT HOME

Memorize Psalm 23 so you can say it out loud, especially at times when you are worried or feel afraid.

Shepherds
Create paper sheep, hide them around the church, and invite a class of younger kids to find them. Say a cheer of celebration when all of the sheep have been found!

Witness

WORDS

shepherd: person who looks after sheep

pasture: grazing land

witnesses in the world

Name some people who are
"good shepherds"
in their jobs.

How do these people care for
their "sheep"?

How can you be a good
shepherd to someone?

<< **Looking Back**

What does the Good Shepherd do?

Prayer
Closing

Use the words of Psalm 23 to pray together, remembering that Jesus
is our Good Shepherd.

12 Jonah's Decision

EXCUSES, EXCUSES!

WHAT IS THE MOST INGENIOUS EXCUSE YOU'VE USED TO GET OUT OF DOING SOMETHING?

DIGGING IN

What would you do in each of the following situations?
Will your decision affect others?

✳ There is a substitute teacher in your classroom, and some of your classmates have agreed to switch names for the day.

✳ It is opening day for a popular new movie that your parents don't want you to see. You are home alone and a friend invites you to go.

✳ You are at a sleepover the night before a big game, and your friends want you to stay up all night.

Bible Text
Jonah 1–4

Key Verse I called to the Lord out of my distress, and he answered me. Jonah 2:1

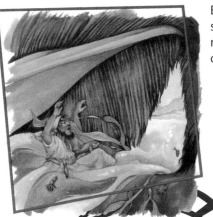

Each of these phrases describes a situation in Jonah's life. Can you number these phrases in the right order?

Land ahoy!

Nineveh, here I come!

Under the fig tree

The runaway

Smells fishy!

FISHY!

Bon voyage!

Man overboard!

Bible Connections

Read about some other biblical characters who made excuses when God asked them to do something. What were their excuses? What did God do?

Exodus 4:10-16
Jeremiah 1:6-9

FAITH Traits

obedience In the Bible: When Jonah disobeyed God, what happpened? When Jonah obeyed God, what happened?
In your own life: When is it difficult to obey God? When is it easy?

Following God's Call

God called Jonah to preach to the people of Nineveh. At first, Jonah refused and ran the other way. What do you do when you hear God calling you to...

Pray

Read the Bible

Help with chores at home

Be nice to someone who has hurt you

Be selective about your TV viewing

Befriend someone who is unpopular and lonely

Encourage your friends not to say nasty things about someone else

BRAIN Builders

BIG Idea

God always knows where we are.

Zookeepers
Give a short presentation (to visitors at the zoo) about the fish that swallowed Jonah.

Poets
Write a funny poem about Jonah (for example, you might start, "Jonah, was it smelly / In the fish's belly?").

Game Lovers
See who can catch the most fish (paper ones!) by sucking them up with a straw.

eMail

Today's Jonahs are those who speak God's message, even when it is difficult and risky to do so.

What are some things that happen in our world that displease God? What might God's message be in these situations?

What are some things that happen closer to home that displease God? Will you speak out against these things, or will you run away? What will you do?

TAKE iT HOME

Draw a fish symbol on your hand to remind yourself to obey God.

Witness WORDS

casting lots: A way to make decisions by using small stones or similar things— like drawing straws or throwing dice

Closing Prayer

Lord, thank you for your great mercy. Help us to be as merciful to others as you are merciful to us. Amen

<< Looking Back

Who helped Jonah rethink his decision about going to Nineveh?

49

Musical Quiz

Draw arrows to show who might sing each of the following songs.

1. All around the World
2. It Is Well with My Soul
3. Be Known to Us in Breaking Bread
4. Come Out of Darkness
5. Catch the Fire
6. Be Still
7. Enter In
8. Higher, Higher
9. He Has Clothed Us with His Righteousness
10. All Creatures of Our God and King

a. Tailor
b. Firefighter
c. Mother
d. Pilot
e. Baker
f. Tourist
g. Shoemaker
h. Zookeeper
i. Host
j. Electrician

Digging In

When do you feel happy?

When do you feel sad?

Bible Text
Luke 1:39-56

Key Verse My soul magnifies the Lord, and my spirit rejoices in God my Savior.
Luke 1:46-47

BIG Idea

God brings joy.

FAITH Traits

joy *In the Bible:* The words *rejoice* and *joy* appear many times in the New Testament. How did Mary express her joy?

In your own life: What is the difference between happiness and joy? How do you express great joy?

Bible Connections

Mary's song is based on Hannah's song, which is found in 1 Samuel 2:1-10. When did Hannah sing her song?

Mary's Song

Luke 1:46-55 is a song of praise that Mary sang when she went to visit her cousin, Elizabeth, after she learned that she was going to have Jesus, God's Son, the Messiah. What exactly did Mary sing about? Discover more by completing these verses with the words listed here.

lifted   scattered   favor   mercy   helped   hungry

- ❧ v. 48 (God) looks with _ _ _ _ _ on his servant.
- ❧ v. 50 (God's) _ _ _ _ _ is for those who fear him.
- ❧ v. 51 (God) has _ _ _ _ _ _ _ _ _ the proud.
- ❧ v. 52 (God) has _ _ _ _ _ _ up the lowly.
- ❧ v. 53 (God) has filled the _ _ _ _ _ _ with good things.
- ❧ v. 54 (God) has _ _ _ _ _ _ his servant Israel.

If you heard wonderful news like Mary did, what would you do?

AMAZING NEWS

MARY SHARED HER AMAZING NEWS WITH HER COUSIN, ELIZABETH. HAVE YOU EVER RECEIVED AMAZING NEWS? WHO DID YOU SHARE IT WITH?

IMAGINE THAT TODAY'S STORY HAPPENED IN YOUR TOWN! HOW WOULD MARY TRAVEL? WHERE WOULD THE TWO WOMEN STAY?

WHAT WOULD PEOPLE SAY WHEN THEY HEARD THIS AMAZING NEWS? WHAT WOULD MARY DO TO PRAISE GOD? HOW WOULD MARY AND ELIZABETH CELEBRATE TOGETHER?

TAKE IT HOME

Memorize Philippians 4:4— "Rejoice in the Lord always; again I will say, Rejoice."
This week, make an effort to rejoice always!

BRAIN Builders

Artists
Create a picture or a sculpture that expresses joy.

Historians
Place each character from the Character game where they belong on the Bible timeline.

Actors
Pantomime joy for a variety of occasions (passing a test, opening a birthday present, and so forth), and have your friends guess why you're joyful.

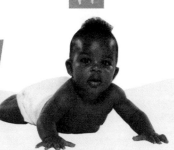

Mary and Elizabeth were filled with joy when they learned they were expecting babies, and they gave God thanks and praise. Thousands of babies are born every day around the world.

Host a baby shower for expectant parents in your congregation. How will you celebrate?

<<Looking Back

Who did Mary go to see after the angel visited her?
Who brings true joy?

Witness WORDS

Magnificat: the name given to Mary's song (Luke 1:46-55)

Closing Prayer

Thanks be to God for joy! Amen

What's in a Name?

Who named you?
What does your name mean?

DIGGING IN

What are the three most wonderful things you have seen, heard, or experienced?

How did you feel as you watched or heard or experienced these things?

What did you do?

Bible Text
Luke 1:57-80

Key Verse Then his father Zechariah was filled with the Holy Spirit and spoke this prophecy. Luke 1:67

John Is Born!

Zechariah and Elizabeth were old and childless when an angel of the Lord appeared to Zechariah and told him that Elizabeth would have a son, and his name would be John. Zechariah doubted the angel and was struck mute.

verse 57: What happened next?
verse 60: Who named the child?
verse 63: What did Zechariah write on the tablet?
verses 64 and 67: What happened to Zechariah after his son was born and named?

I wonder what it was like to realize that God could do something that seemed impossible...

Bible Connections

Songs have been used for thousands of years to offer praise and thanks to God. Zechariah knew his psalms well! Check out Psalms 41:13; 72:18; and 106:48; and then look at Luke 1:68.

BIG Idea

Speak the news— celebrate God's gifts!

FAITH Traits

thankfulness *In the Bible:* With the birth of John, many Old Testament prophecies were coming true. What did Zechariah do to express thanks to God?

In your own life: How do you thank God?

WORDS

Benedictus: the title of Zechariah's song in Latin, *benedictus* means "praise be"

prophecy: a word or message from God

covenant: a binding agreement between two parties

Wants, Needs, and Thanks

What do you want?

What are you thankful for?

What do you need?

TAKE IT HOME

Keep adding to your list of thanks this week.

BRAIN Builders

Moviegoers
List five movie scenes that show people expressing thanks.

Artists
Make thank-you cards for people who work behind the scenes at church: gardeners, coffee makers, receptionists, custodians, and anyone else you can think of.

Researchers
Discover the meaning of the name of at least one of your classmates. What does the name *John* mean?

Game Lovers
Play What's the Big Idea?

Believe It **OR** Not!

WHICH OF THESE STATEMENTS IS TRUE? FALSE?

Typewriter is the longest word that can be made using the letters in just one row of the keyboard.

"Go" is the shortest complete sentence in the English language.

It's physically impossible for you to lick your elbow.

The smallest bone in the body is found in the little finger.

Have you ever believed that something is false and later learned that it is true?

witnesses
in the
world

What are God's gifts to us?

How do we misuse God's gifts?

How can we show our appreciation of God's gifts?

<<Looking Back

Who named John?
What happened to Zechariah when John was born?

Closing Prayer

Thank you, God, for
my mom. Amen

and Dad

15 The Christ of Christmas

BIG Idea
Jesus is the best gift ever!

Bible Text
Luke 2:1-20

Key Verse To you is born this day in the city of David a Savior, who is the Messiah, the Lord. Luke 2:11

C-H-R-I-S-T-M-A-S

Write down as many words as possible that are connected with Christmas and that begin with one of the letters in the word CHRISTMAS.

DiGGinG in

How many announcements do you hear and see every day?

What are they about?

What is the most interesting announcement you've ever seen or heard?

W

FAITH Traits

harmony *In the Bible:* How do you think the shepherds' lives were affected by their visit to the manger?

In your own life: How does Jesus' birth affect your life? Does the news of Christmas bring peace and harmony to our world today?

Bible Connections

The birth of Jesus saw the fulfillment of many Old Testament prophecies. What did Micah and Isaiah prophesy?

Micah 5:2-5a
Isaiah 7:14

JESUS IS BORN!

If Luke's story of Jesus' birth was the only one you had, what would you know? Circle these statements if they are part of Luke's Christmas story. Where is the rest of the story? (Hint: Look in Matthew 1:18—2:12.)

Emperor Augustus ordered a census.
Quirinius was governor of Syria.
An angel appeared to Joseph.
Jesus was born in Bethlehem.
Herod was king.
Angels appeared to shepherds with the news of Jesus' birth.
Shepherds traveled to Bethlehem to see Jesus.
A bright star appeared in the sky.
The Wise Men visited Jesus.

Why did God choose to tell ordinary shepherds about Jesus' birth first?

Story in Song

Musicians have been writing Christmas songs for centuries. Summarize the Christmas story using the titles or words of well-known Christmas carols. What is your favorite Christmas tune?

TAKE iT HoME

Find ways to celebrate Christmas meaningfully this year by keeping CHRIST at the center of all your celebrations.

BRAIN Builders

Artists
Design a Christmas card in the form of a birth announcement.

Storytellers
Read a children's picture book about Jesus' birth to a group of preschool kids, and encourage them to act it out while you read.

Actors
Pretend you are an angel in your town today. How will you tell people about Jesus' birth?

Puzzle Pros
Complete a crossword puzzle about all the Bible stories you have explored in the past few weeks.

witnesses
in the
world

Name some ways people in your community celebrate Christmas. How does your family celebrate? How can you spread the news of Jesus' birth at home? In your neighborhood? Around the world?

Witness WORDS

registration: a census ordered by the emperor

Bethlehem: means "house of bread"; hometown to King David and Joseph

Messiah: the One promised by God

manger: an animal's feeding trough

<< Looking Back

Why were Mary and Joseph in Bethlehem?
Who learned of Jesus' birth before anyone else? What happened?

Closing Prayer

Lord Jesus, we love you. Thank you, God, for the gift of your Son. Amen

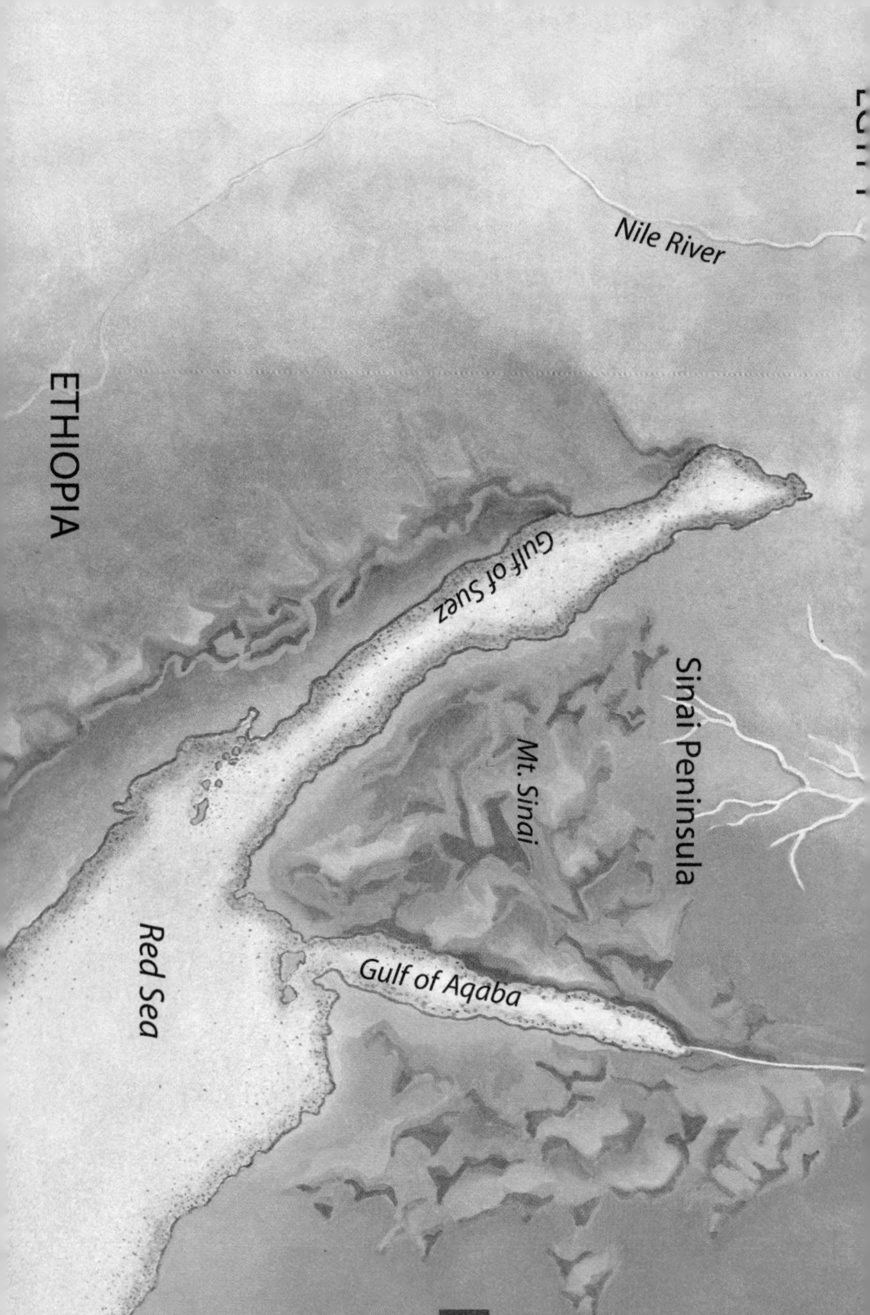

ETHIOPIA

Nile River

Gulf of Suez

Sinai Peninsula

Mt. Sinai

Red Sea

Gulf of Aqaba

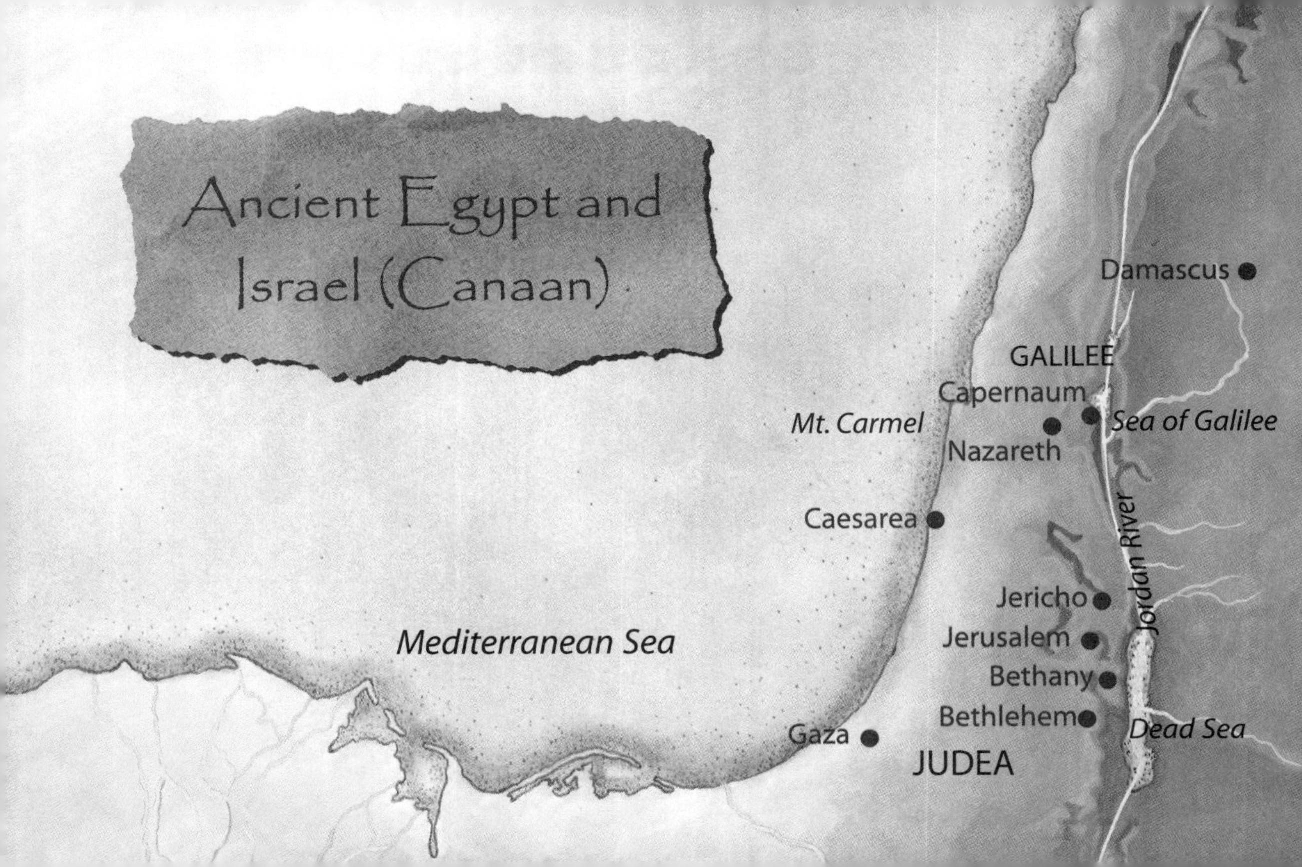

Ancient Egypt and Israel (Canaan)

Mediterranean Sea

Gaza

Caesarea

Mt. Carmel

Capernaum

Nazareth

GALILEE

Damascus

Sea of Galilee

Jericho

Jerusalem

Bethany

Bethlehem

JUDEA

Jordan River

Dead Sea

WHAT'S IN A NAME?

Do you know where your name came from? Do you know what it means? Try to match the names of the biblical characters on the left with the meanings on the right.

1. Adam
2. Eve
3. Cain
4. Abel
5. Joseph
6. Moses
7. David
8. Samuel
9. Saul
10. Solomon
11. Elijah
12. Esther
13. Jonah
14. Mary
15. Elizabeth
16. Zechariah
17. John
18. Jesus

score 10

craftsman
God gave
vanity, breath
the perfect one
Savior
God is my oath
star
of the earth
drawn out of the water
dove
peace
memory of the Lord
my God is Jehovah
life
may Jehovah add
asked of God, heard of God
asked, demanded
beloved

Answers:
1. of the earth, 2. life, 3. craftsman, 4. vanity, breath, 5. may Jehovah add, 6. drawn out of the water; 7. beloved, 8. asked of God, heard of God, 9. asked or demanded, 10. peace, 11. My God is Jehovah, 12. star, 13. dove, 14. the perfect one, 15. God is my oath, 16. memory of the Lord, 17. God gave, 18. Savior